THE TAO
OF ARCHITECTURE

THE TAO
OF ARCHITECTURE

Amos Ih Tiao Chang

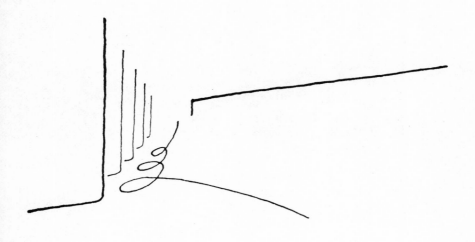

PRINCETON   UNIVERSITY   PRESS

Formerly titled *The Existence of Intangible Content in Architectonic
Form Based upon the Practicality of Laotzu's Philosophy*

LCC 80-8677
ISBN 0-691-03963-1
ISBN 0-691-00330-0 pbk.

Printed in the United States of America by
Princeton University Press, Princeton, New Jersey

First PRINCETON PAPERBACK printing, 1981

FOREWORD

The wisdom of an ancient culture infuses and illuminates this book. Expressed in modern terms, Mr. Chang's work is unique in its revelation of the vitality of intangible elements in architecture. For all who begin to realize what a barrenness of spirit has overtaken their present efforts, Chang offers a simple medium, as clear as spring water and as natural as air, in which the architectonic imagination may again build without loss of breath and courage. Creative forgetfulness is Chang's phrase for it.

A. M. FRIEND, JR., A.M., LITT.D.
JEAN LABATUT, A.I.A.

CONTENTS

NOTE ON THE ILLUSTRATIONS. The Chinese paintings are reproduced in this volume through the kindness of the Freer Gallery of Art, Smithsonian Institution, Washington, D.C.
Clearing Autumn Skies over Mountains and Valleys, detail. Ink and tint on silk, attributed to Kuo Hsi; Sung dynasty, 11th century.
Pavilions, detail. Ink outline on paper, attributed to Li Kung-lin; Sung dynasty, 11th-12th century.
Realms of the Immortals, detail. Ink outline on paper, attributed to Li Kung-lin; Sung dynasty, 11th-12th century.
Palaces Among Mountains, detail. Color and gold on silk; Ming dynasty, *circa* 1500.

THE TAO
OF ARCHITECTURE

INTRODUCTION

PHYSICAL MANIFESTATIONS of life are plastic and when they fail
to suit the requirements of time and place they may be manip-
ulated and changed by man. But that which is intangible is
beyond the power of man, existing as a permanent reservoir
from which the potential of life may be drawn as the need arises.
Beyond the power of manifestation, this unseen factor usually is
not only unseen but tends also to be unappreciated. In particular, it is in Laotzu's philosophy that this factor is so funda-
mentally emphasized.

Ours is a time of material progression and rapid differentiation. For this reason, it seems that two particular problems in
the realm of architecture worthy of note and vital in practice
are the human quality of physical environment and the harmony
and unity of different buildings. As time passed, it appeared
clearer and clearer to me that it is Laotzu's active negativism, the
philosophy of intangibility, which might give some answers to
these two problems.

> "The Tao that can be told is not the permanent Tao;
> The names that can be given are not the permanent names." [1]
> (CHAP. 1)

Laotzu is fairly well known in the west today. Unfortunately,
since his ideas are expressed in the form of simple paradoxes,
their meanings can be easily misunderstood in terms of tangible

[1] All the quotations are translated from Lao-tzŭ's Tao-tĕ-ching. (Ssŭ-
pu-ts'ung-k'an, Commercial Press edition, Shanghai, 1929, vol. 307)

3

names and words, which are regarded as harmful by Laotzu himself. In the above quotation from his book, Tao-te-ching, he lays down the foundation of his thinking by saying that tangible presentations, particular names and words, have their preconceived meanings, but changing associations according to time and place render these meanings sterile. Regarding reality as what we think it is instead of as what it is, Laotzu develops every variation of his thinking according to relative viewpoint, the theme most brilliantly presented by his follower Chuangtzu:

> "Limited by space, a frog in a well cannot
> understand what is an ocean;
> Limited by time, an insect in summer cannot
> understand what is ice."
>
> (FROM THE ESSAY "AUTUMN FLOOD")[2]

Yet, Laotzu's conception of relativity is in an organic sense. To gain and to lose are regarded as parts of one thing. In one example, Laotzu describes the organic change in nature in terms of the changing form of a bow which is widened when its ends are pushed closer. A layman can understand relativity better through knowing the changing form of a bow. In many other paradoxical examples, Laotzu gives a truer picture of life as an interchanging and flowing experience in which nothing could be permanently held or absolutely known.

> "Without allowance for filling, a valley will run dry;
> Without allowance for growing, creation will stop functioning."
>
> (CHAP. 39)

Since growth is regarded as the basic function of everything alive, anything which is complete, perfect, and cannot grow and change is by definition dead. Laotzu's idea of life and of the function of nature is that all things are springing from nothingness, growing from incompletion toward their fullest maturities, and thereby becoming deteriorated. Aware of this eventual and inevitable deterioration and the invalidity of the absolute value

---

[2] Chuang-tzŭ, "Autumn Flood," Nan-hua-chĕn-ching XVII. (Ssŭ-pu-ts'ung-k'an, Commercial Press edition, Shanghai, 1929, vol. 536, VI, p. 10)

of any tangible being in terms of names and appearance, he suggests affirmatively that the way to face reality is to be content to accept the negative side of being as well as the positive side, and to leave completion to nature.

The wisdom which reveals this insight is: since any aspect of reality is only what we think it is from a certain viewpoint and has no real definite being, there is only self-contentment and not self-sufficiency in any conceivable being existing in human life in particular and nature in general. It is by containing the non-being as a positive means that self-contentment could become self-sufficiency. With regard to humanity as a whole, therefore, Laotzu is for modesty, tolerance, and impartiality. Yet, ironically, even over-assertion of his philosophy may fail us. Regarding non-being as an absolute end, his follower Chuangtzu goes to the extreme of this line of thinking and is so indifferent to the difference between a beginning and its corresponding ending in anything as to deny the process of life itself. This viewpoint which amounts to a philosophy of total non-existence is beyond the power of many to grasp. From the position of an architect of our day, I am interested in accepting from Laotzu the practicality rather than the conventionally interpreted philosophy of inactivity in life as a whole.

It is interesting to note, however, that Laotzu does not limit the application of the process of growth and change to any particular realm of nature. The Tao, the general intangible being of creation, manifests itself in physical, biological, and psychological substantiations of which in each case the Te is the intangible being of the particular manifestation. The clarification between these two intangible beings (one provided for all and the other given to individuals) convinces us that things are created equal (all from the oneness of Tao) but different (specific manifestations of Te). Beyond the mere implication of infinite plurality of specific genera in humanity, the idea of non-being suggests that physical and psychological manifestations are as lively as biological ones because nature is an organic whole in which terminological and homological demarcation is temporary and untrue.

"Reversion is the action of Tao.
Deficiency is the function of Tao."
(CHAP. 40)

To understand Laotzu's idea of nameless process of change, consequently, it is necessary to know that it concerns the opposite states of being and non-being, not the tangible states of being in terms of name and appearance. Thus, death is considered as only the non-being of life similar to the state of life before birth. The intangible being of a thing, therefore, may be interpreted as that which is the obvious complement to the "thing," giving it inter-related and reversible oneness and full reality. Whiteness and blackness are suggested as opposites because eventually the eye which looks on white tries to supply black as a balance. More specifically, Laotzu implies that ignorance and intelligence are opposites because through subjective enlightenment or objective revelation, extreme intelligence or wisdom will produce impartiality and amount to deliberate ignorance.

In any case, according to the relative point of view, what is called positive is merely the end either conventionally emphasized or specifically expected. If white be called positive in one place in contrast to black, it could also be called negative when black is valued from another viewpoint. Or, according to the degree of manifestation, we may say that the tangible aspect of a thing is positive and the intangible aspect of a thing negative. The order could be reversed.

This order of reversion appears realistic to us when we relate the principle of Laotzu to the interaction between any conceivable pair of opposite states of "things" in nature. We will see that, as exemplified by the interdependency between male and female, every individual thing has its insufficiency, the negative and intangible content.

This intangible content in "things," though not materially manifested, is regarded as something REAL. In Laotzu's text, it is called the "formless form" or the "intangible phenomenon" (Chap. 14). As vague as it seems, to grasp its reality, one need only think of a female image in a man's mind or vice versa.

6

Similarly, one pole of a magnetic field or an acid is not self-sufficient and has its intangible opposite. The meaning as well as the vitality of "things" in biological, physical, and psychological aspects exists in the combining of a pair of obvious opposite beings, each not having the attributes of the other and each needing the other.

The basic idea of Laotzu's thinking is, as has been said, that once the point of tangible fulfilment is reached, the potential of growing is exhausted. He speaks for a factor which by its intangibility leaves an almost unbounded possibility of change for further development. This general point is most powerfully expressed in terms of the constituency of physical space:

"Moulding clay into a vessel, we find the utility
   in its hollowness;
Cutting doors and windows for a house, we find the utility
   in its empty space.
Therefore the being of things is profitable, the non-being
   of things is serviceable."

(CHAP. 11)

This statement in relation to architecture suggests that the immaterial, that which is likely to be overlooked, is the most useful. Void, conventionally regarded as negative, actually is more important because it is always capable of being filled by solid.

But physical void as such is still meaningless to us because although physically man, an everchanging being, lives in space, psychologically he lives along the dimension of time. Time, although intangible, is more intimate to man because it is more sensible within human organism itself and primarily makes up the continuity of life. Consequently, with or without conscious consideration, architectural composition is based on the time factor for both physical function and psychological experience. With time as the main factor of organization, architecture could be defined as "spatial expression of human life and experience in time."

7

Probably it is due to human consciousness of temporal limitation of life that organization of living space cannot exclude the somehow ambiguous maxim of "Convenience." One way to clarify this ambiguity is to assume that a minimum amount of time for circulation is desirable and therefore when circulation frequency is high, distance must be short enough to compensate for the shortage of time. Thus, when circulation speed is constant, a functional space which is more frequently used and absorbs more circulations should, comparatively, be placed closer to the center of circulation of a composition.

By so reasoning, we see that of two classrooms of the same capacity, the one which is continuously used on a one-hour basis probably needs more centralized location than the one which is used, also continuously, on a two-hour basis.

But let us consider an element which is only periodically or contingently used.

> "Although a sage travels tiresomely all days,
> he never leaves the burden of his provision cart."
>
> (CHAP. 26)

It is true that, primarily, Laotzu is aware of the liability of tangible provision and is for sufficiency in simplicity. Searching further in the domain of intangibility, however, we also find his awareness of simplicity without unpreparedness. To him, as suggested in the above statement, the thing not being used is usable and a thing which is not tangibly occupied could be considered, to a certain degree, as being intangibly occupied.

It thus becomes logical to assume that the location of a functional space in a composition is determined not entirely by actual frequency of use, but also by the desirable potential preserved for unforeseen service. To justify the central location of a firehouse in a town, for example, one has to imagine that moment after moment an intangible fire engine is leaving, though actually it is kept unmoved. It was by considering what is not being used as a part always having real function that Tokyo Imperial Hotel was saved from a fire.

8

An unused allowance of time-space occupancy in a composition is what makes it possible for a man to move in architectural space without any time limitation. Without this intangible content, readiness, functional space would become rigid and devoid of life quality.

It is possible that by comparison of potential service frequencies of different functional spaces, a framework for the functional organization of a composition could be specifically established. At the moment, the estimation of intangible service frequency of a functional space, particularly when various organization levels are involved, is so intricate, so arbitrary that it can be judged only on the basis of experience and in accordance with specific viewpoints and conditions. For this reason, the problem of functional organization will not be dealt with in further discussion.

Even so, the aspects involved in the problem of psychological experience alone are many. As an architect, I am limiting the scope of this investigation to cover the area that an architect should consider in visual composition. Because the profundity of Laotzu's thinking lies in its simplicity of reasoning, however, it requires analogical thinking to arrive at an understanding of the possibility of using his ideas in dealing with so many trivial as well as important matters in architectural composition. It is by analogy, alone, that the all-embracing principle of Laotzu's philosophy is utilized as the main structure of thinking for this investigation.

Through non-formal contemplation, I am inclined to believe that it is the existence of intangible elements, the negative, in architectonic forms which makes them come alive, become human, naturally harmonize with one another, and enable us to experience them with human sensibility. This is the basic viewpoint of this investigation.

Since according to the principle of relative viewpoint an architect must not be subject to an absolute rule, this investigation deals mainly with intangible content as the means of a composition. The principle of using negative means (intangible content) to achieve positive end (what is expected) originated from Laotzu. However, I must be held responsible for the specific interpretations and the suggested methods in connection with the application of the principle.

The material of this investigation has been accumulated by direct experiences with architectonic forms. These experiences consist of many intricate and moving images existing in the mind, the domain which is always beyond tangible representation. The result of this investigation, therefore, can exist in its fullest reality only in the minds of those who apply the principles involved in their own ways.

NATURAL LIFE-MOVEMENT

IN ARCHITECTURAL VISION

*"Nature eliminates surplus and compensates
for deficiency."* (CHAP. 77)

NATURAL PHENOMENA appear meaningful to us not only when
we interrelate their momentary existences but also when we
synthesize the temporal changes among them from a certain
viewpoint. This is a point particularly important to Laotzu who
thinks that reality is only what we think it is and what counts
in understanding nature is the process of its function by which
alone the law of existence supposedly designed by some unseen
power could be revealed.

This does not mean that one has to believe in God by name.
In Laotzu's simple language, the supernatural being is something
unknown. The only thing intelligible about it is its function
as manifested in the process of becoming, from the intangible
being to the tangible being, of any conceivable aspect of reality
such as the obvious rhythm between life and lifelessness.

*"Longevity belongs to those who die without
losing their lives."* (CHAP. 33)

Making no reference to God or the soul, Laotzu implies
directly another intangible aspect of human life. In reading this
statement, one would think that life could become encourag-
ing if we regard physical non-existence as an infinite part of life.

Laotzu's philosophy, as climaxed in the above statement, regards nature as an organic whole in which the intangible part is

11

the most vital. The individual is asked not to be blinded by momentary or fragmentary states of being, but to be aware of what is not seen yet destined to come. Putting himself at the core of total natural manifestation, he is looking at "things" divergently through the transparency of time. He thus not only sees the "things" but also the indefinite states of change among "things" and the power of infinite growth inherent in the realm of intangibility. Without mentioning the polarities of change by name, he generalizes the process of change in a simple statement:

"Nature eliminates surplus and compensates for deficiency."
(CHAP. 77)

With the suggestion of this statement in mind, one sees that before we put any architectonic form in space, there are various natural attributes waiting to transform it. The tangible means of composition at man's disposal are limited, the transformations offered by nature are countless.

Man's experience in space includes smell, hearing, touch and the interrelated sense of temperature and humidity. All these will contribute to man's sensation of distance between his position and the sources of sensations. None of these sensations, however, is as important as that of vision. Whatever a normal man senses, specifically or compositely, through other physiological agents, is complementarily associated with and confirmed by visual form. Confronting so many problems of sensation, an architect is particularly responsible for what and how a man will see in relation to the tangible elements which, directly or indirectly, stimulate all other sensations, giving him a feeling of existence in space.

Nevertheless, seeing is not a matter to be accomplished by man alone. Man himself only opens his eyes. It is light, one attribute that man lacks, which raises the curtain of external reality for him. The relation between man's experience and light in nature is an organic change between the tangible and the intangible because, as Laotzu puts it, "Nature is eternal because it does not manifest itself." (Chap. 7) While our eyes

12

are immersed in a sea of millions of color-light-rays, we can experience colors only indirectly through prismatic refraction and reflection from pigments. During the process of seeing, furthermore, man is actively passive in adapting himself to different degrees of light intensity; nature is passively active in diffusing its intense sunlight with vapors and dusts brightening the shaded areas by negative reflection. All these states of adaption or modification, from deficiency to compensation or from surplus to elimination, are parts of the natural life-movement in architectural vision.

"The way to acquire positive is to contain negative."
(CHAP. 28)

The concealment of colors and intense brightness in natural light is meaningful. "Colors can blind," says Laotzu. (Chap. 12) Focussing our eyes on something intense in value or chroma, we will, when time passes, experience a negative halo. When black and white or contrasting hues are in proximity, this experience of negative image will fuse with the actual values or hues, which are already modified by the action of contrast, and destroy the physical form defined by them. Thus clarity is lost. Curiously enough, it is because of the presence of a certain amount of the intangible (greyness) in colors that clarity is naturally preserved. Nature conceals itself not only to preserve the potential of its energy but also to preserve man's capability to receive its energy.

Greyness or colorlessness is, as illustrated respectively in a color wheel and a prism, the eventual and original reality of colors. It is negative in appearance but decidedly positive in potential. It is not seen as color, but it *is* "colors."

Negativism in color, consequently, means that whenever a color contains greyness, it has its intangible content of its opposite and thus is capable of harmonizing with its opposite at ease. Furthermore, the more greyness a color has, the more it loses its tangible being and the more variety potential it has. While harmony of tangible colors is a complex process beyond rationalization, total or partial greyness in color can always serve

13

as a medium for intelligent linking and fusing of many colors. It is natural that nice colors are called "shades."

Human organism is created to receive the negative side of nature. It receives reflected light better than the light itself, the glare. The portion of this reflected light manifested to man is also limited, particularly when pigmented surface is included in a lighted field of vision.

Because of the presence of light, color can be said to have two obvious aspects, constant color and apparent color. Comparatively, the former does not lose its identity under normal condition and possibly is the result of mental interpretation founded in experience. The latter is our immediate experience of it as modified by abrupt change of light.

Reluctant of superfluous harshness, nature provides another intangible element, shade, to preserve what is expected by mental constancy on one hand and to enable us to see without being intensely stimulated by apparent colors on the other. By elimination and compensation, a strong light will transform a color, but a seemingly useless dim light will protect its constancy with softness. What could be over-stimulating and distracting thus retains integrity in its tender but nevertheless steady exposure.

> *"Harmonize with its light,*
> *Sympathize with its dustiness.*
> *This is the way of natural unity."*
> (CHAP. 56)

Nature as a temporal being never stops its changing from one extreme of being to another. The natural diffusion of sunlight may not exist in clear weather as we expect. Under the pressure of shining light, a polished surface will reflect what it receives and reduce the genuineness of an actual composition. If a shining image is the effect wanted, of course, shining also would be regarded as a means of composition. Unfortunately, the expected quality of a building in the long run should be considered as well. As exemplified in most of the historical build-

14

ings, it is rusticated materials having the quality of natural weathering which will stay longer, not the finished and artificial one. They outlast the surfaces artificially finished because their rough, weary and perplexing quality has the power of tolerance to cancel the menace of time. The formation of the mellow beauty of old rusticated buildings has its simple but profound justification in the philosophy of non-being.

The immediate function of negativism in surface finish is even more important. Besides its contribution of settling dusty elements in its minute voids, rusticity has the power to pierce the sharp shining of light and reflects it in its partial area, making it fused with the shadows concurrently created and giving the surface a vibrating quality. The harsh light in nature thus is softened by material we usually borrow from nature.

Light, color and texture combined give surface quality. Any surface quality itself, again, has no difinite being unless it is compared with another surface quality. Since in both conception and perception, white is not white without the existence of black, the same kind of greyish surface will appear brighter in contrast with black but darker in contrast with white. What is lacking in one thing is always compensated in another thing. They then will complement each other by natural or artificial light. That which is facing the light source will be reduced in brightness by aerial diffusion. That which is hidden in shadow will receive light from negative reflection and be brightened. None of them, nevertheless, can eventually remain itself and avoid becoming dull greyness within human organism. It is because of the natural rhythm of fatigue and relief that a total harmony of surface quality externally accomplished could be intermittently maintained in man's internal reality.

The partial concealment of light is not provided for acquiring constancy and harmony of surface quality alone. When spatial form is concerned, nature again is for incompletion. To manifest either a rectilinear or a curvilinear form, it is necessary to have light unevenly distributed. Along the dimension to time, nature also is functioning on the basis of incompletion. A basic rec-

15

tangular form with different recessed surfaces will be enriched only through the organic decomposition created by different shadows at different times. As a whole, the void enclosed by this form will be seen as dark in day time and, negatively, bright at night. All of these life-movements for definition, for enrichment, and for the general rhythm of work and rest are created by deficiency in lighting.

Light, natural or manufactured, floods to every corner of an architectonic form. Darkness, which is preserved, is what makes depth be seen. If light be called the life-blood of an architectonic form, darkness could rightly be called its soul.

As to the experience of spatial extension itself, our eyes are not able to see everything in a visual field all at once. Clarity of an object at one distance is accentuated only at the expense of the blurring of objects at another distance. This deficiency of our visual organism is a natural asset. Without blurring, the buoyancy of intermittent change between clarity and obscurity would not exist.

The efficiency of our visual organism is so low that even objects facing us at similar distances are beyond our power to grasp at once. Except objects made familiar through experience, visual elements perceived by us at one instant are limited to only a few. It is the natural picture frame, the emptiness surrounding an unfinished manifestation of physical reality, which makes a momentary being integrated and induces man's fluid continuity of clear vision in time. It is so because human mentality, as a part of unfinished nature, is provided for the experience of unfinished existence.

At this point, it is necessary to say that visual objects are not as static as we might carelessly think they are. Actually they have life. They have life because their existences are complementarily inter-related to and influenced by each other; because they are subject to transformation due to the transfusion between brightness and darkness, and because they are experienced by life.

It is hard to say how much surface quality contributes to the visibility of an object because size and distance are the more obvious factors of visibility. As a whole, however, it might be acceptable to say that both surface quality and size are playing a part and that complementarily they create a total impression seen from distance. When surface quality is impressive by contrast with the brightness of a neighboring object or objects, apparent size could be small. To keep the same amount of impressiveness when surface quality is less impressive, apparent size must be enlarged. They are cooperating on the function of visual manifestation which requires one of them to be passive. In architectural composition in particular, form usually takes command and surface quality is complementary.

Nature is for minimum means and maximum end. As a natural product, our small eye is constructed for distorted vision of large scope. So primarily what we immediately see is not the actual thing existing in space but the retinal impingement of objects of which the apparent sizes are horizontally and vertically reduced when distance increases. Beyond the power of compensation by binocular superposition, this inherent distortion has its deficiency yet to be overcome.

Our motion in space and past experience helps us to understand that an object of normal size actually is bigger than what appears in our immediate perception from a certain viewpoint. From time to time, by the proportion to the size of the human body and conventional elements such as a door, the objective conception of a rectangular framework is gradually established. Despite the fact that physical space actually is geodetic in construction, we conceive architectural space mainly on the basis of this idea of rectangularity. This conception is so influential that perspective reference given by planar indication experienced from a limited number of viewpoints can give us a realistic, though temporary, sensation of three-dimensional space.

It would be mechanical, however, to interpret perception and conception separately. It would also be incorrect to emphasize one aspect at the expense of the other. Following the line of Laotzu's thinking, they must be organically related. In this case, the positive end expected is the rectangular formation of the reference points of objects existing in physical space. Immediate perception received at a certain distance is something incomplete and has its intangible content.

> "Greatness means vanishing;
> Vanishing means distance;
> Distance means return of greatness."
> (CHAP. 25)

In Laotzu's thinking, gain and loss are always in balance.

18

What is vanishing in space implies the increase of distance. Inversely, what is decreasing in size has the potential of becoming great.

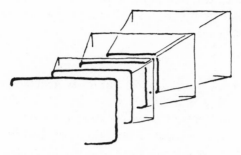

Consequently, if we plot the traces of transformation from the perception to the conception of one section of a form, such as a rectangular plane, the resultant form of the traces would approximately become a "negative perspective," which is intangible. The potential of becoming great of an object, furthermore, is proportional to its distance from us. The farther it is, the greater its potential to grow.

Experience of physical space is a matter neither of perception nor conception, but the interaction between them. This process of growth from deficiency to compensation brings inherent movement to physical form.

This intangible content of size does not manifest itself. When the mind tends to interpret size as diminishing in distance, an object of parallel form with limited perspective influence is experienced as tending to grow outward instead of being diminished in space as it would appear in mechanical projection. This effect is particularly obvious in our experience at intimate distance of a vertical form. In this case, the diminution effect in immediate perception due to short distance in horizontal direction is strongly over-compensated by mental interpretation derived on the basis of long distance in vertical direction. Naturally, the interior of a cathedral or the exterior of a skyscraper will be experienced as vitally opening up toward its height.

19

Vision from a stationary viewpoint concerns size and distance. Vision in motion concerns speed and time as well. Stationary as the limited number of visual objects are in relation to the earth, their passiveness makes it possible for man to experience the infinitely multiplied visions by change of direction and change of sequence.

Any existence occupies time, but no existence persists in time. When the speed of motion is high, the mind will be occupied by preceding objects and not capable of accepting a new independent image. A simple composition will thus be experienced as a complex one instead. On the other hand, no matter how complex a composition is, its complexity will not always clearly exist in the mind when it is experienced by us at leisure. Seeing slowly, one will naturally free himself from the after-image or even the memory of preceding visions and be ready to receive new images.

When time serves as the container of visual impressions, simplicity is enriched in vision at high speed while complexity is lessened in vision at slow motion. From a humanitarian point of view, complexity in a subway tunnel and simplicity in a prison are both undesirable.

Primarily because of this limitation of our mental capacity, visual objects existing in space are bound eventually to become non-existent to us after we are fatigued by the monotony of the same object. Our change of visual interest superficially is created by the attraction of a new object, but actually is brought about positively by the negative factor, fatigue.

But visual objects with tangible variety are only attractive and not always directive to the fatigued eye because our sequence of seeing them is rather arbitrary. One may be attracted by any of many visual objects, but he will naturally be invited to look through or toward an empty and vanishing field. Our reluctance in seeing a monotonous object will only push our sight aimlessly away from it, while an empty solid can always definitely repulse our sight at a nearly predictable angle. Everything else being equal, it is deliberate provision of emptiness which will secure the expected direction of our seeing process.

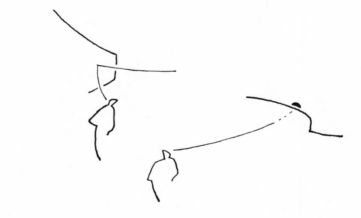

The same effect of direction also exists when a known or expected object is partially or totally hidden behind an empty wall to induce our attention to penetrate through it. In emptiness and beyond emptiness, there is unfulfillment of expectation or curiosity to suggest definite direction. Nature itself is functioning on this basis of growth from non-being to being. Unreal as emptiness is thought to be, it serves as the reminder of direction.

Our experience of light and color determines the primary visibility of visual objects. Our experience of size, distance, speed and time, however, determines the visual scale and the temporal meter of a composition in the actuality of which observers will move and see along certain directions created mainly by actual emptiness and supplementarily by fatigue. All these are the inherent potentials an architect could utilize or the prerequisite conditions he should consider for a composition.

However, the full meaning of existence is beyond the power of any manifestation. What appears tangible, architectural or natural, is only a means to suggest that which is lacking in appearance and existing in man's intangible understanding and aesthetic feeling.

VARIABILITY AND

COMPLEMENT

"Completeness without completion is useful.
Fulfillment without being fulfilled is desirable."
(CHAP. 45)

BESIDES functional, economic and social considerations, the natural conditions covered in the preceding discussion limit an architect's freedom to a certain area of action. Direction of the sources of light and its intensity will limit his choice of surface quality and form; sight distance will control the visual scale of composition and the pace of life of the occupants will pre-decide the temporal meter or degree of elaboration.

An architect does not have the same temporal control enjoyed by a musical composer. In many circumstances high and low speed of motion, either actively or passively performed, must both be considered. Since sight distance from an architectonic object is varied, an architect does not enjoy the freedom of a painter either. In no case can he assume that lighting will be fixed in intensity, direction and timing.

Under so many varied conditions, the only thing an architect can do before the start of a composition is to assume only the most probable, not the possible, lighting conditions, sight distances, viewpoints, speeds, and certain routes along which the occupants will travel with functional purposes.

Visual elements in an architectural composition include everything which will come into an observer's eye. Individually, some architectural elements such as a wall pattern are pictorial; some, such as a fountain, may be sculptural. Conversely, actual paint-

23

ing and sculpture could become architectonic when they contribute desirable and coherent quality to help define a space. Architectural or otherwise, visual elements become architectonic only when their tangible meanings fade and they remain as the parts in a harmonious whole. Interrelatedly, however, any individual object is usually integrated with different groups of other objects and variably become many partial compositions. The points to be covered are countless. Analysis in terms of tangible names would require endless discussion.

To simplify our study, visual elements are abstracted despite complex constituency. Mainly according to increase of the length of visual duration at similar sight distances and supplementarily according to increase of sight distance, visual elements in a composition are classified into the following levels: line, planar shape, single mass, attached masses, environment (enclosure) and conceptual continuity.

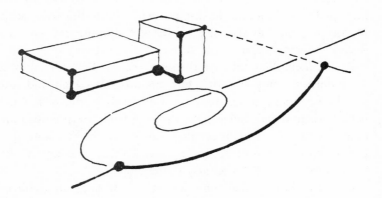

The temporal sequence arranged by an architect is objective in a sense and never could conform to the subjective motion of an observer. Fortunately, the human being is able to experience what he sees conceptually. Sporadic and fragmentary visions are subjectively interpreted and organized but nevertheless always referred to objective reality for confirmation. Neither subjective nor objective experience is independent and complete in itself.

Following the organization levels, mentioned above, in the mind of an observer parts are integrated to become a whole and smaller wholes to become a larger whole. Each time the organization level is elevated, either according to sequence or according to scope, the content of a unit is enriched with the variety of smaller units and the fusion of the many surface qualities they carry.

All these units can be seen in one image, but environment is something beyond that. One has to have the experience of being surrounded before he realizes the existence of such a state. It is at this level, nevertheless, that the expression of architecture reaches its maturity. Light, color, line, shape, solid form and balance of solid forms will be compositely experienced as the inter-related contents in one composition. In a more extensive scale, this experience of composite variety reaches its fullest development when man's successive memories in different environments are mentally composed into a symphonic whole. This whole, analogously speaking, has its timbre in color and texture, its pitch in size and its loudness in contrast of brightness. Its formation, however, is materially governed by natural setting and human needs.

"The finest has no shape." (CHAP. 41)

Either in microscopic or telescopic observation, the growing and living part of nature is seen as composed of infinite elements irregularly but flexibly integrated by nothingness. Their formation changes periodically according to change of time and change of our viewpoint. Anything that appears to our bare eye, therefore, is not the real thing but the already integrated whole of some sort. But idealism has no real being either; point, line, plane and volume are intelligible to us when they are indirectly defined by other entities presumedly existing in void. What exists in physical space could not even have temporary being without our conceptual interpretation and what exists in our mind would have no meaning without reference to physical formation.

Dealing with physical objects, an architect conceives what is intangible through tangible form. To him, a point would mean a minute but perceivable area such as the top of a nail, a line would mean only a linear inference such as a joint, which actually has width. Similarly, shape, volume, etc. are physical beings defined by minute areas and inferred lines.

To conceive or to perceive, the knowing of reality is a matter of realizing the inter-transformation and the necessary inaccuracy between what is existing and what is non-existing.

Laotzu's idea of formation is heavily concerned with emptiness or non-existence. To him who regards nothing as persistent, what is essentially important in things is the possibility of becoming something, not the opportunity of remaining as something confronting deterioration. Consequently, meaningful incompletion is taken as the most desirable state of tangible being.

While conjecture may blind insight to things, an impartial but active attitude may lead us to see truer beings. A conscious comparison will reveal the fact that a complete circle will be distorted in perception and might be interpreted as elliptical. A section of this circle, on the other hand, probably will be interpreted, because of our desire of the least effort in apprehension of simplest form, still as "a section of a circle." Everything else being equal, it seems that a shape consisting of disconnected sections, rectilinear or curvilinear, can convey its real being better.

The point which is more important is that a fragmentary shape has the potential to grow, to become a finished entity in our mind. A complete one appears static, rigid and lacks vividness because it allows no room for the growing mind to function.

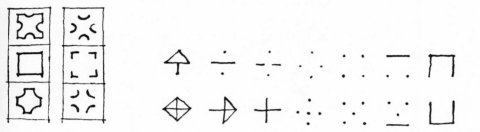

Consisting of intangible content, an incomplete or fragmentary shape preserves the possibility of flexible adaptation to match with neighboring shapes of the same organization level as well as to be integrated with them to become a grown unit of larger scale without destroying the continuity of their background. To grasp the reality of harmony and growth, one has only to look upward at night to see the stars, which do not manifest their inter-relationship themselves, to find out how well those floating points match with any man-made form.

Since everything is relative, even the being of void is not definite. It only suggests something empty, less manifested or merely less distracting. Living space becomes nothing and empty only when we take it for granted that the existence of air is natural and deserves less consideration. Relatively, but consistently, void could be defined as something occupied by nothing and solid as something surrounded by nothing. Functionally, void without solid would mean return to nebulous wilderness. Visually, solid without void would mean loss of visible form. Neither of them could exist without the coexistence of the other.

But nature is always jealous of perfection. When the moon reaches its fullest form in our eye, the deficiency of a waning moon is bound to follow. It so appears as partially hidden only

27

to reveal its momentary perfection to others in another place. Similar to the moon, which moves in relation to the earth and the sun, architectonic form also is passively experienced as moving when an observer moves around it. From various points of view, an observer may synthetically experience the complete extension of a geometric form, such as a hemisphere. As an architectonic form, however, a hemisphere usually is designed mainly to be seen from the ground. And from a certain point of view on the ground, it appears to us as being flattened. Its own completion thus brings depreciation of its completeness. Only experience from several viewpoints can overcome this visual deviation.

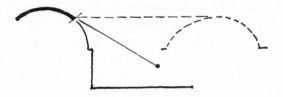

But an architect cannot always expect an observer to see from different viewpoints. So, often he has to assume that it is necessary to reveal an architectonic form to an observer who will see it from a particular angle. This is possible only when the form is incomplete, penetrable and seen as inter-related from inside to outside.

Primarily created to satisfy functional requirements, architectonic forms are evolved by assimilation of smaller units such as pieces of bricks each of which, when unrelated to each other, has no elaborated form nor direct function. These uniform and seemingly insignificant units, however, have the virtue of passiveness to ease the process of physical integration. When solids for definite functions are required to be placed together, the problem of integrating solids of different forms arises.

Fortunately, while solid forms may not merge with one another, the infinite variations of conformity inherent in void can always serve as a medium to relate them without or with very little, physical contact. The basic technique of architectural composition seems to be so simple.

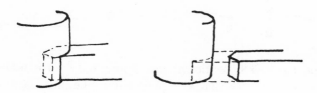

If man were free from the penalty of weather, architecture would remain at the level of furniture design, the art which mainly concerns integration of medium-sized solids by void. Regrettably but fortunately, nature never provides enough for us. Instead, it contains insufficiency in its provision demanding the art of architecture to spring up and grow in the form of space containment.

Space containment is a means rather than an end. Overuse of this means would bring stagnation to space and isolate man from the stimulating attributes of nature. Its formation, similar to topographic precipitation, demands solids or static elements to be located at places where void for fluid movement least is needed.

Void itself, like spiritual life itself, is beyond vision and audition. To be consistent with the theme of intangibility, it seems that though temporarily man has to protect his physical being, he must not deny the eventuality of life, physical decay. He must, therefore, not be afraid to accept the fact that his final and original beings exist in void instead of in solid. We may say that emphasis on solid is disharmonious with the recognition of spiritual being. In fact, like the spiritual being of human life, void is something not only real but also infinite. One cannot say,

29

for example, that when there is an increase of three inches in the spacing between two chairs, there is an increase of three inches in void. It means something more than that. To the occupants of both chairs, actually there is a total increase of six inches from two viewpoints.

Solid by itself is restrictive and deadly, but void is infinitely inter-penetrable and has the potential to become something much more than its superficial quantity. No one can estimate the length of spiritual life. Similarly, no one can estimate the service that might be rendered by a common void in time as experienced by millions of human eyes.

To an architect whose composition is beyond physical function, reduction of solid or preservation of void has its aesthetic contribution. As an empty being itself, void could become various forms in its dependency on solid. In analogy to musical composition, solid is playing the treble part to crystallize architectonic melody, the seeming emptiness of void is inherently and coherently playing the harmonic accompaniment without any tangible shape of its own.

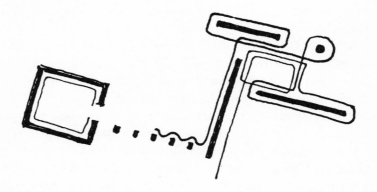

Knowing that mass is for void and not vice versa, one would realize that to reduce the solidity of mass is to enrich the potential variety of void. While a confinement can strike only one single note, a space fragmentarily defined could be "woven" into many harmonious chords by the path of human sight.

"*Long and short will manifest each other;
High and low will attract each other.*"

(CHAP. 2)

Laotzu's idea of the relationship of things concerns the growth and change between them. This is apparent in surface quality, or brightness contrast which, as has been mentioned, has no definite being itself. It becomes a certain thing at a certain moment only by being in contrast with another thing existing either in immediate coexistence or experienced association.

As demonstrated by the counter-balance between the two sides of a balance, things are comparable by pairs and any specific aspect of anything is intelligible only by measurement of variation between two extremities. To be precise, the phenomenon of contrast in spatial form should be defined as sensory difference of two things between two obvious opposites.

When this difference is perceivable at one sight, natural proportion similar to the proportion of the heights of average male and female gives a mild vitality to a composition. In any composition of architectonic forms, however, it is the existence of a familiar scale comparable to man's bodily size, his stride of walk and the binocular displacement formed by the visual lines of his two eyes which makes the physical size of an object convincing. Naturally, rigid proportion as a definite being without comparative relationship with human scale will only lead to misapprehension.

It is difficult to know how architectonic forms are compared

31

in size because length, area, and volume come into our experience almost concurrently. We may, however, assume that size is seen as a three-dimensional profile along which visual liveliness is initiated by the effect of negative perspective. When man's sight is moving horizontally, the change of height is more obvious. When his sight is moving vertically, the change of breadth is more impressive. In both cases, depth seems to intensify the liveliness of vision by vibrating focuses along the third dimension, in which, usually, overlay gives a duet quality to a composition.

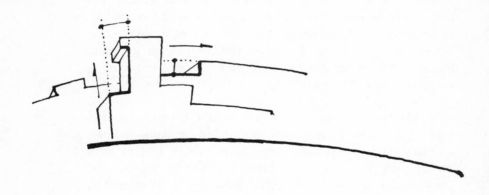

But analogous to value in color, size is only the primary attribute of architectonic form. Like hue in the case of color, shape serves as the secondary attribute of architectonic form.

Since none of individual things has definite being unless it is manifested by another thing having the obvious opposite characteristics of its own, a curved shape acquires its meaning through its contrast with straightness. With this conviction, a general survey will reveal the existence of at least three conceivable polarities of shape, namely: horizontality and verticality; perpendicularity and obliquity; and, curvilinearity and rectilinearity. Simple or compound, minute or colossal, architectonic forms are experienced as varied combinations of these elements, the hues of form.

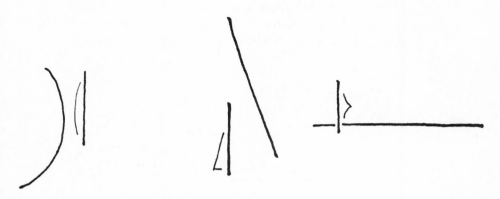

The more vital reason that these three polarities can be regarded as basic is that the components in each polarity have the power to influence each other. When an arrangement of two parallel straight lines is in proximate position and enclosed by two curves, the straight lines will be deformed and appear to be bent. Similarly, when two lines are in immediate relationship with a third line, the one which is in oblique position with it will influence the one of perpendicular position to tilt and counterbalance each other. In a lesser degree, a long horizontal element also has the tendency to influence a vertical one to lean in such a direction as to balance the approaching action of the horizontal. Similar to the interaction between contrasting hues in color, opposite shapes in each pair have the potential to transform their opposites toward a complementary effect.

Because of the natural rhythm between fatigue and relief, the transition of our sight from one tangible shape to another contrasting one existing in the neighborhood gives man the clarity of perception, attraction of interest, and inducement to movement. All these effects of refreshment, however, are more efficient when transitional void between opposite shapes is provided. In all cases, moreover, the mental vitality created by contrast seems to explode and then to evaporate in void. The stronger the contrast, the greater volume of void to receive this explosion is needed.

But interest and movement stimulated and created by contrast in void requires concurrent or continuous existence of two shapes; its lively quality is not self-contented in immediacy.

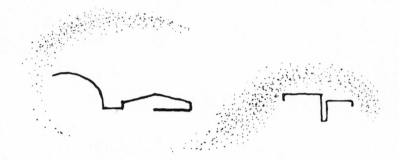

When we see a form along a tangible line, we seek for immediate references along this line. When our sight is traveling in void, it jumps from one definite point to another. Comparatively, for the reason that our eyes will feel more relieved in emptiness, the path of our sight has a stronger tendency to traverse from point to point in void than along a tangible line. For this reason, the power of negativism may again be utilized to achieve further richness without unnecessary complication.

"The way to allow for fulfillment is to concave." (CHAP. 22)

With this quotation in our mind, we see that an architectonic form consisting of concave curve also has an intangible straight line adhering to the two ends of the curve. We also see that around a polygonal form there is an intangible curve swaying from one apex to another which inevitably implies a cylindrical form. Nature manifests these phenomena with good reasons: In the first case, a concave curve furnishes passive resistance against

34

wind load; in the second case, the ease of fabrication in rectilinear construction usually cancels the desirability of acquiring
maximum space by minimum perimeter for a perfect cylindrical form.

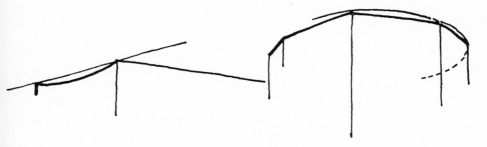

A study of the relationship between obliquity and perpendicularity will show the same complementary effect. A wall with a reversed batter will automatically give an intangible line in perpendicular relationship with some reference point on a level
ground. A cantilever roof in perpendicular relationship with a
wall surface, as a result of lighting and sanitary reasons, suggests
an oblique line between the eave and the wall footing.

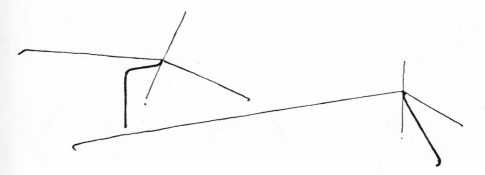

More obvious than the two polarities mentioned above is the
complement between the horizontality and verticality. When a
vertical form is of light construction and when a number of its
cantilevers are repeatedly superimposing one another, our sight

35

is strongly induced to travel vertically rather than horizontally. Conversely, repetition of obvious verticality will lead to an inducement of horizontality.

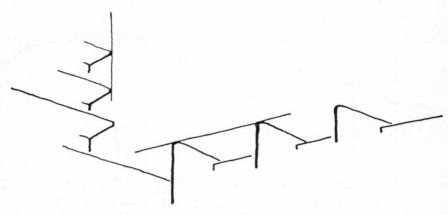

It seems that the function of intangible complement tends to furnish the opposite of a tangible shape. If the chords of a polygonal solid are concave inward and each is curvilinear, the immediate reaction we would have after we see it is the experience of a series of short straight lines in a polygon formation. And, after further experience in our mind, these intangible segments will mentally grow again into a cylindrical form. Similar to our experience of color, the negativism of successive reactions is true in our experience of any shape that has a conceivable opposite.

By concavity in relation to our position in space, a form not only acquires complementary richness for itself, but also creates the harmony between its intangible shape and the tangible but similar shape in another form. The function of harmony given by this intangible complement is more lively and vivid than harmony in terms of tangible similarity. One can easily visualize that if a series of bells is hung between two horizontal elements in proximity with a vertical element, the lively quality of the harmony between tangible verticality and intangible verticality created by repeated horizontality will be substantially reduced.

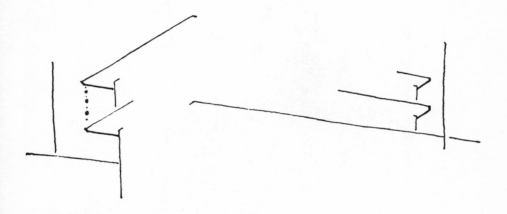

Since any aspect of reality is only what we think it is, it is not necessary to limit ourselves to the domain of tangible means and assume that concavity should be created by a single tangible line. Simple or compound, concavity could be of any constituency because what counts in a composition is the intangible shape created by the relationship of points, not the tangible form to define these points.

When we have this assumption in mind and assemble the three basic polarities so far intelligible to us in a "relationship circle," each polarity would have its "complement area" between the perimeter and the core of this "relationship circle." Near the core of this "relationship circle" where opposites have equal and intermingled manifestations, individual shapes will be cancelled by opposites and both are neutralized and together become homogeneous. Similar to intermediate hues in color, prob-

37

ably, intermediate shapes along the perimeter of the "relationship circle" would be the tangible mixture of two closely similar shapes.

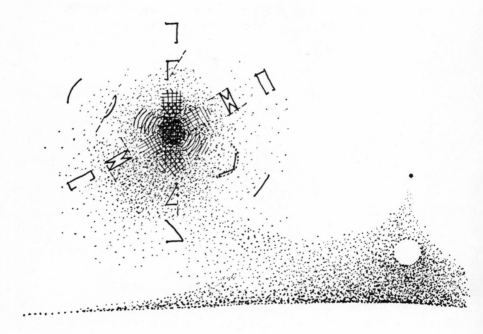

If the primary attribute of form, size, is added to this "relationship circle," it could become a "Form Attribute Cone," which appears to parallel closely a color cone. The most obvious phenomenon of analogy between them is: when value in color is increasing or decreasing, hues become less and less manifested; when apparent size is decreasing or increasing, shapes will also lose their identities.

As the means at an architect's disposal, size is the "value" of form, shape its "hue," and the degree of concavity its "Chroma." Convexity is analogous to full saturation in color and hence impermanent. Homogeneity of intermingled shapes is analogous to grey in color and capable of serving as an empty background.

Like greyness in color, concavity supplies complementary shapes and hence allows for easy transition between contrasting solid forms. It also serves as a link overlapping the form of solid and the form of void harmoniously embraced by solid.

Playing the two important roles in architectural composition, fragmentariness and concavity respectively furnish variability and complement to enrich form. What one should be aware of is that any richness, when used as a means to emphasize a dominating element, is something to reserve and not to assert.

"Scarcity has the power to gain." (CHAP. 22)

The above statement is understandable since any kind of treasure would have no value if it is available in large quantity. Comparing a crowded city and a tall and slender solid surrounded by a tremendous volume of natural space, we will see that while space is valued in the former, solid is emphasized in the latter. Similarly, to elaborate the whole facade of a building means to flatter the importance of a simple doorway and to keep the whole facade plain means to treasure a decorated entrance as a diamond jewel.

It is for us architects to remind ourselves that on a piece of white paper covered by a large area of black, it is the border meagerly left untouched which will be seen better.

BALANCE AND EQUILIBRIUM

"The way to be is not to be." (CHAP. 24)

ARCHITECTURAL COMPOSITION primarily calls for a happy combining of similarity and difference. The former furnishes ease of apprehension and, because of uniformity of construction elements, is what an architect can easily have. The latter creates change and interest but, because of functional and material limitation, is what an architect ordinarily lacks. Usually, change or interest in architectural composition depends much on the intermittent change between uniform shapes and empty spacing to give rhythm. Sometimes, when a building is independent and of extremely simple form, individual form has to contain its own attraction by direct contrast with a surrounding volume of void commensurate with the vitality created by the impressiveness of the form.

However, when aesthetic delight is specially required, other means for enriching an architectonic form are not lacking. Besides the inter-compensations of natural attributes, there are contrast of size and shape and complement by concavity at an architect's disposal. All these are means to achieve visual richness arranged under the general principle of fragmentary parts for flexible whole, the principle which requires the architect's technique of handling points for composing line, lines for composing plane, and planes for composing volume.

But regarding a composition as a more extensive whole, difference and similarity created by contrast and complement are

41

only one aspect of architectural composition. They create only the primary visual sequence.

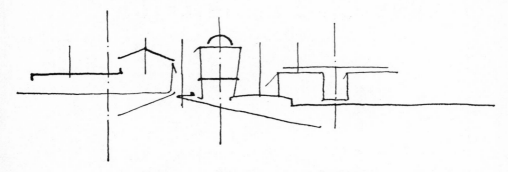

Consisting of visual elements of different organization levels and modified by many natural attributes, an architectural composition in space is always a complex one. The interrelated contrast and complement makes this complexity become more intricate and necessitates sequential adjustment in a more extensive sense to simplify complex elements of a composition by means of unification.

Unlike other visual arts, architecture is an art of life itself expressed in life-size scale. Visual elements as the means of an architectural composition, therefore, are not only something to attract interest and to induce movement, but also essentially to create restfulness in which the potential of life, work and human continuity are embedded. This quality of rest and recreative potential is made visible in architectonic form in terms of balance of mass and equilibrium of environment. They make man feel at ease, stable and in a state of relieved satisfaction for a certain length of time. It is the intermittent combinations of these feelings, ease and stability created by balance and equilibrium, which control the secondary and tertiary sequences in architectural space. Without it, transitional motion created by contrast and complement would lead to endless action and eventual fatigue. Among these two, balance of mass usually is minor and controls sequence of shorter duration.

42

Balance of mass is a compound being. It has its physical aspect as well as its visual aspect. And any attribute in one aspect will influence the state of the other. The basic principle of physical balance seems to be provision of ample resistance against possible loading. To refine the application of this principle, loadings are accumulated from various directions and concentrated on few supports. When the potential of materials is high, a building built of these materials becomes hollow and the size of materials becomes visually not representative of the force required to transfer or to resist the loading. Theoretically, as exemplified by a balloon, force could be formless.

Man's liberation from the heaviness of masonry and his knowledge of synthetic application of new materials and new principles make him understand that a solid section of a member means stress, its depth means better resistance against bending, and two members acting on one joint may mean but one force. He also realizes that in many new materials, size does not mean weight as we would think in seeing traditional masonry. In short, we know that construction is not structure.

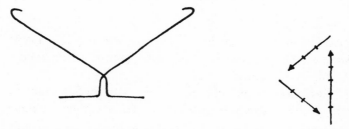

Construction is tangible but not necessarily what it appears to be. Structure is intangible and never is fully manifested. In fact, we are living in a field of gravitation forces without our consciousness of its existence.

Investigation of structure instead of construction will show that basically the creation of all architectonic constructions are based upon one simple principle, namely: provision of the minimum of available material to resist the maximum of possible loads. While construction methods change, structural principle remains the same.

But unlike pure engineering where the objective is efficiency and economy in construction, architecture is something deeper. It aims at emotional satisfaction as well as physical integrity. It is a language which has the emotional power to express with authority the structural meaning of a functional space.

Physical space calls for a factor of safety in structure. Every joint, every bay, and every building is designed on this basis. The factor of safety required in each case is different, but it is always greater than unity. The allowance for intangible and unpredictable loading in physical structure is usually exaggerated, but man counts on this unused provision so that he may live in a space without fear.

The recognition of this intangible state of safety is not a matter of surface consciousness. To pronounce it with accent, to reveal as lively a trustworthy structure, allowance for growing and counterfusion of structural meaning must be contained in architectonic form.

"The way to weaken is to strengthen." (CHAP. 36)

Realizing the eventuality of sharpness is fragility, Laotzu is aware of the non-being in things. To him, this principle is applicable in any aspect.

Positive expression of structure usually gives instantaneous assurance by extra heaviness. But after a certain moment of man's visual experience, this positive expression is bound to become a static impression and even may lead to our disbelief in the strength of materials. Either a solid or hollow pyramid form belongs to this category of positive expression. Its characteristic is: structure and construction have the same proportion of resistance and loading. It lacks the allowance for complement and is devoid of life.

To generalize the methods of lively expression in structure, we may assume that a structure is expressed through the interaction between its supported part and its supporting part. Also,

44

we may assume that in either acting or resisting, force is visually presented in terms of size, form movement, and material quality.

To clarify our thinking, let us assume further that the resistance and the loading of a structure are each treated as a whole and respectively represented by their readings in Y-axis and X-axis in a coordinate diagram. Plotting a line from the origin to a point which ordinate represents resistance and abscissa, loading, the slope of this line, which represents the factor of safety, will be greater than unity.

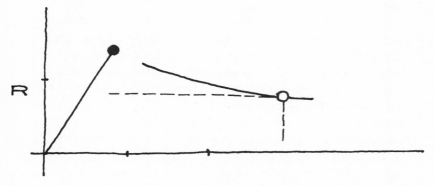

A vital way of structural expression is not to manifest this safety immediately but to contain a certain amount of apparent weakness by which, alone, the growth of strength in mental experience is induced. This means that the slope of a line representing our immediate impression of a construction is less than unity. Our experience then moves from the coordinate point of apparent risk to the coordinate point of actual safety.

The most usual instance of such an arrangement is that in which structure is expressed by placing the thinner sides of a series of buttresses, in consistency with physical reason, toward the observers. When we assume that loading is constant, the front view of these buttresses will give an immediate impression of weakness, but the revelation of their depth either by shadows or by being seen from the sides will manifest their actual size and strength. Through size variation, respect for actuality thus is growing in our mind and mental interpretation will move

45

from the point of apparent risk to the point of actual safety. Often, such allowance for mental growth is achieved by partial hiding or even total concealment of the resisting members.

In some other cases, growth of resistance in our experience is initiated by material quality. This is particularly effective when metal is employed and sizes are diminished by reflection from polished surfaces whereas the strength of material is enhanced by this metallic quality of reflection. What is seemingly weak at first sight becomes something light but nevertheless having its intangible strength.

As to the supported part of a structure, usual practice emphasizes the horizontality of its bulky form and the floating quality of this bulky form by enclosing enough quantity of void between solids. If we keep resistance constant, in such a case, loading is diminishing in our experience. What is seemingly heavy at first sight becomes something bulky but light. In a similar way, the apparent heaviness of a solid wall can be mentally reduced by actually being broken down into parts. Often, form movement is applied in the opposite way. When the apparent size of a supported part implies excess of lightness, downward movement is needed for compensation. In all cases, reduction of mass is desirable for the expression of both the supported part and the supporting part of a construction. By reduction of mass or creation of void, at the lowest level of visual organization, a raked joint expresses ample resistance against loading rather than the state of being squeezed.

Structural expression by containing intangible content means apparent heaviness in the supported part of a structure and apparent weakness in its supporting part. Through the suggestion by size variation, form movement, or material quality, an observer will experience the light bulkiness in apparent heaviness and the strengthened lightness in apparent weakness. This method is thoroughly applied in the construction of traditional Chinese architectonic form in which a bulky roof is visually raised in void by the movement of its curling form and its light columns are strengthened by color contrast and their context with a solid terrace.

46

Expression of structural tenacity means control of an observer's experience of the form from its non-being in construction to its real being in structure. The objectives of this method are: bulkiness without heaviness; lightness without weakness. The amount of apparent risk contained in an architectonic form for suggesting the real safety of its structure and creating the feeling of physical balance depends on the availability of time for man's visual experience in space. Dramatic expression in a busy place and timid conformity in a place of leisure are both beyond reality.

Physical balance seems to come first to the mind of an observer. Afterward, the size, the form movement, and material quality will coherently influence the visual balance of a composition. At the same time, light, shades, shadows, colors and even the observer's state of mind all play a part attributing to a total effect. The precise relation of the component factors in visual balance is beyond analysis.

We have to assume that the study of visual balance is something dependent upon perceivable size and the general relationship of masses of similar density.

Any independent form, architectural or natural, exists in space in a state of balance. It appears in balance to us mainly because of three factors: first, man's consciousness of an axis of balance which serves as a reference of adjustment; secondly, the quantity of masses and the distances of their centroids from the axis of balance; and thirdly, man's position of observation and judgment in space.

Architectonic form has no definite outlines. It may be as simple as a box, but it also may be a composition of physical and visual inter-relationship among parts, a complicate group of masses juxtaposing and overlapping one another in different directions.

Complex as a group of attached masses is, we can always abstract them into two general categories, symmetrical and asymmetrical. The former could be schematically represented by a simple and single geometric form, the latter, by two simple geometric forms with one extending more horizontally and the other less so from their axis of balance.

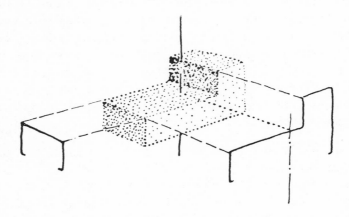

Physically mass is three-dimensional. Its centroid exists in the midst of mass and is usually hidden from man's sight. Abstractly, man resolves this actual centroid into two component axes perpendicular to each other within a rectangular framework. And, because architectonic form is manifested by light principally coming from a single source, the area to be covered for conscious adjustment of balance is limited to one side of a three-dimensional form. As a result, the visual balance we experience from any viewpoint is the adjustment of an axis to balance the obvious areas of a three-dimensional profile or the adjustment of the obvious areas to become balanced in relation to a specific axis.

"Standing tiptoe a man will fall.
Striding astray a man cannot walk."
(CHAP. 24)

Throughout Laotzu's text we see his emphasis on the non-being because, to him, no definite being can survive change unchanged. What he is looking for is not the remaining state of things, not to be one way or the other, but to be adjustable between two extremes and thus always be in the state of intangi-

48

ble balance. For him, the quality of lively form is neither definitely symmetrical nor definitely asymmetrical.

Mechanical interpretation of the balance of an architectonic mass can cover only the momentary being of its position in space as seen by an observer from a certain viewpoint. When time and the viewpoint of the observer change, anything in balance will change its state from another viewpoint. A simple horizontal and symmetrical mass with a flag pole as its visible axis will be seen from its front as symmetrical and in balance. But one also can see that this same mass attached with the same tangible axis will become off-balanced when it is seen from oblique position. The reason for this deviation is simple. At the level of perception, the areas on the two sides of the tangible axis in foreshortening impression will not remain equal.

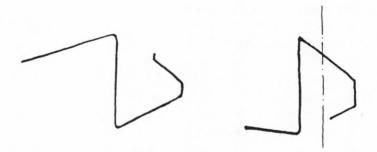

Only the incomplete being of symmetry can save symmetry from being deviated when judged from different angles. In the above example, it requires the disappearance of the tangible axis. Playing the part of intangible content of symmetry or the allowance for becoming asymmetry in this horizontal form, this invisible axis is adjustable according to variable balance of perceived areas seen from different angles. It injects life-quality into the symmetrical form but does not reduce the symmetrical quality of the form when it is seen from the front.

Similar to the above example but converse in relation is a case of vertical mass with its baseline. While a tangible base symmetrically attached to the vertical mass will become unequal and cause the vertical mass to appear as tilting, an intangible one is always adjustable to fulfill variable requirement of visual balance.

The adjustable balance of a symmetrical form is made possible by containing intangible axiality, either in the form of an intangible axis or intangible baseline. To meet this requirement in actual composition, uniformity in the middle part of a horizontal form and commensurate emptiness at the base of a vertical form usually are desirable.

As to the balance of an asymmetrical form, the conditions of its being in intangible balance are just opposite to that of a symmetrical form. In an asymmetrical form, a tangible axis is usually non-existing and always adjustable according to the viewpoint of an observer. Yet, when man sees it from its front, he is not satisfied to interpret it as in balance on the basis of inverse proportion of level-arm and weight. Dynamic symmetry as such in terms of mass alone creates only the feeling of off-balance rather than otherwise.

What is lively must be similar to life itself. We may borrow an important rule of balance from the anatomy of a zoological being, man in particular. As a finest product of nature, man's body is in a state of balance when his arms and his legs are in a position to be moved effectively to compensate for position changes of the body. To allow for this free compensational change of man's bodily position, empty space usually is preserved so that his body may move freely into a new supported position.

When this simple rule is applied to the balance of building mass, our conscious review will show that an asymmetrical form usually has some empty space preserved at the less extended side of the axis of balance. It is so not only because the building mass at this end is tall, more important, and needing empty space through which its top could easily be seen, but also because the intangible and opposite pose of the building mass in relation to the visual axis has its implied position in space. When both

50

the tangible and intangible poses are considered as parts of a composition, naturally man will sense the axis of balance as existing in the center of the combination of his visual image and mental image experienced from the front. The feeling of off-balance is thus materially eliminated.

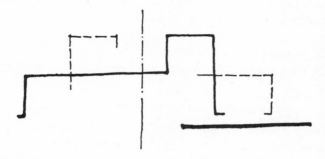

This simple rule of asymmetry without off-balance is applicable in the arrangement of either large or small scale, but it is not always necessary. Other factors in visual organization may reduce the requirement of preserving empty space at the less extended end of an asymmetrical form to the extent that in some composition in which full front view never appears, provision of this empty space is totally arbitrary.

Individual form, symmetrical or asymmetrical, usually is not existing in space alone but is deliberately incorporated with other individual forms. The transference of an observer's sight from one form to another is in a state of wavy movement in which contrast between symmetrical form and asymmetrical form or rhythm of either furnishes vitality, which in turn is pacified by the intangible balance of each form. The stability and the restfulness compositely created by physical and visual balance thus furnish an obvious temporal mark of man's visual sequence in space and prevents his visual interest from being exhausted.

After being relieved from continuous motion by concentrating his attention on the balance of one mass, man's visual energy will be restored and his attention will be attracted into emptiness and then to another object. Partly because of complementary contrast of form but partly because of the contrast of surface quality, the movement between two consecutive balances spans over divisions of smaller visual sequences. With so many visual attributes accumulated from light, color, shape and balance surrounding or being contained in it, an environment is already rich in its solid melody and harmonic accompaniment in void.

Up to this point, we confront the problem of human quality in the environment (enclosure), the basic aim of architecture.

"The greatest has no boundary." (CHAP. 41)

That which is growing never has a limit. Unfortunately, an environment becomes intelligible to us only when we are conscious of its physical confinement or, in a lesser degree, when we experience its visual definition. In many cases, our experience of an environment is arrived at by both.

In contrast to mechanical matter, man is always a flexible being. Wherever possible, he stretches his arms, moves, jumps and swings in space. Whenever possible, he also grows. The contour formed by his bodily movement and growth is an elastic volume of void to which no physical form can ever precisely conform. Unreal but so true, this elastic volume of void is what we really live in. It has no boundary. Yet, its formless form is an indispensable field in which life takes form and flourishes.

Since it is nearly impossible to have a conditioned space without physical boundary, the elasticity of this formless form could be only meagerly preserved and suggested by flexible space deliberately provided. Laotzu's emphasis on contentment within allowance of becoming has its reason in every aspect. Following this idea of contentment, our search for this flexible space shows that it exists in the margin between the boundary of physical confinement and that of a space visually defined. Architecturally, it means that when there is a small rug whose size is smaller than the room, the atmosphere of flexible growth in the room will be strongly felt.

This does not mean that the physical confinement should always be large enough for deliberate contraction of a visual space. A door may be unnecessarily double in size, but if it is not provided with a visual margin, an observer would always have the feeling of being limited in a mechanical boundary. On the other hand, no matter how limited the size of a door is, if ample margin for visual reference is provided, one will feel free within the allowance of the margin and be guided to go through it comfortably. Size does not necessarily count in architectural space. It is the growth of size which is vital.

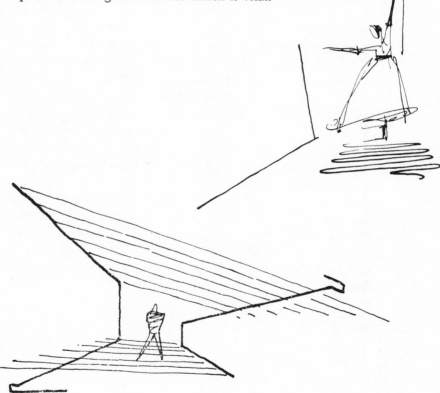

This suggestion for growth of space by deliberate contraction probably has its highest success in an interior canopy. Cutting space horizontally, it suggests the growth of height by its lowering from the ceiling on one hand, and the growth of width by its inward contraction from the walls on the other. By contraction, a small room may become psychologically spacious, a road with a shoulder of inferior pavement may be felt as widened. The same principle is applicable to an environment of any scale. Hesitation to accept the significance of contraction created by a moat, a flower bed or a picture moulding is indeed regrettable.

But in creating the feeling of flexibility, what really counts is the indefiniteness of the physical confinement, not necessarily its physical elasticity. There are compositions which require only visual and not physical spaciousness. So often this is achieved by eliminating the visibility of physical confinement. Since nothing has definite being, the condition to satisfy this requirement is the disappearance of visible definition rather than compliance with the theory that certain brightness creates certain spaciousness. Observation will show that in a sea of darkness or dim light, a black ceiling will disappear and enlarge a space while a white ceiling, a being which could be carelessly mistaken as always of spacious quality, will become more visible and reduce the spaciousness of space instead.

A fully reflecting surface is particularly useful in such a case because it has no definite being of its own. It manifests so many and claims no particular status in space. Putting two full-sized mirrors on two opposite walls, one will see that their endless counter-reflection will make a room's visual size infinitely enlarged.

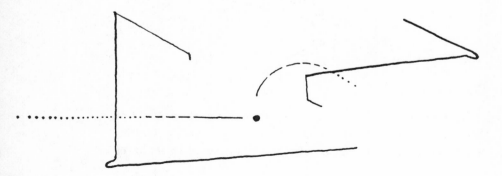

Non-being is always infinite and useful, but artificial creation of non-being is always difficult and expensive. Fortunately, it is always possible to provide a recess at the edge of a ceiling or the footing of a wall. By so doing, a defined space is made visually to lose its definition. Our experience of the elastic volume thus is an outward growth from the boundary of physical confinement to an unseen boundary expanding to an unfathomable limit.

One way or the other, the compactness without restriction created by contraction of visual space and the spaciousness without expansion created by visual unlimitedness are important qualities of living space. They create equilibrium between confined and defined spaces and can be easily achieved if we understand the importance of the principle of non-being.

The elasticity of space created by the interaction of defined and confined boundaries is the human factor within a single environment. As a result of fragmentary integration of each environment, physical limitation partially becomes non-existent and directed space between environments is created.

The term "flowing" is commonly used to express the action in a directed space. By flowing is meant the action of our sight when it is guided to travel from one enclosure to another, by invitation of emptiness in void as well as by repulsion from or penetration through the emptiness of mass.

The factors determining the process of seeing in flowing or directed space are many. From time to time, we should be aware that contrast and complement of light, color, texture, shape, and balance all play a part to attract our interest and contribute to the total sequential effect of action and repose in our visual experience. Also, we must admit that sequential effect given by the total visual content of an environment is variably modified by the personal state of mind of an observer.

Everything else being equal, however, flowing in directed space is mainly created by the contrast of openness between two consecutive environments in the conceptual continuity of our memory and is complementarily guided by solids parallel to the direction of flowing. Interrelatedly, an open environment has more room for bodily and optical motion and will absorb more attention, a narrow environment probably will give an impression of congestion and accelerate forward action. In both cases, guidance by solid form seems to confirm the direction of flowing but nevertheless serves as a rhythmatic link between two separate or interpenetrating volumes of surrounded void.

But separately, openness alone suggests uncontrolled expansion and enclosure alone suggests compressed stillness. The extreme of the former will lead to exhaustive action and eventually unmeaningful fatigue while the extreme of the latter, outright lifelessness. Some means are needed to curb open space from flooding and to relieve enclosed space from stagnating.

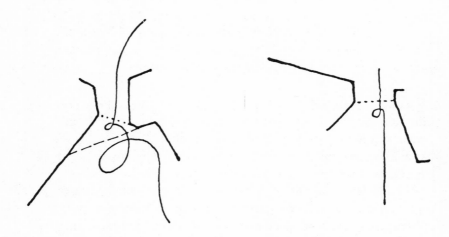

Liveliness always needs the potential of becoming. It seems that one way to curb flooding in space is by holding an environment together by an intangible line suggested by tangible mass which is in perpendicular relation with the direction of flowing. The result achieved by this arrangement is an effect between being and non-being of flowing. Man's sight will thus follow the perimeter of the environment, then temporarily be halted from crossing the estuary of the environment by an inferred line and, finally, it will swing back to cross it once the inertial curb is overcome. This effect is equivalent to a "retard" in music. It holds man's sight in suspension and thus prevents it from evaporating itself in endless action.

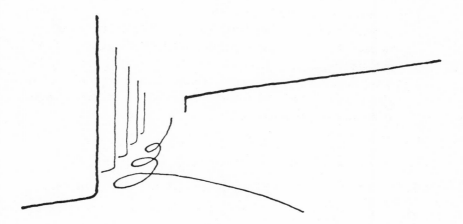

An opposite situation of equilibrium in flowing space is a case in which an environment is visually confined in almost every direction. The intangible content needed in such a case is the feeling of some opening to relieve the compression. A series of lateral planes, either a row of buttresses or a venetian blind, is one means which could imply the lateral openness beyond them and to lessen the longitudinal action squeezed by lateral confinement. Our sight will thus be successively attracted by the brightness of the lateral planes and each time is tempted to go laterally but always swings back and proceeds to another intangible openness implied by brightness. This is a vibrating effect equivalent to a "tremolo" in music. A rather confined environment hence becomes a visual volume of melting softness.

As more obviously seen up to this point of discussion, either an architectural composition itself or its relationship with other elements needs balance and equilibrium as the means to create the secondary and tertiary controls of man's visual sequence in architectonic space. Both of them will effect the sequential harmony of a composition.

However, it seems that at the level of conceptual continuity, sequential effect usually is subjective. It is always renewed and unfinished. While music is psychologically existing but physically a non-being, architectonic continuity is physically existing but psychologically a non-being. Concerning the highest level of visual organization, it is hard to say where an architectonic symphony starts and where it ends.

INDIVIDUALITY AND UNITY

"Things are the manifestation of being.
Being comes from non-being." (CHAP. 40)

WHEN deliberate arrangement is possible, a building composed of elements in contrast and complement of surface quality and form is integrated with other buildings usually in terms of contrast of balance and contrast of openness. The reason is that what is asymmetrical usually can be more effectively incorporated with what is symmetrical; and, what is confined usually is more desirous of being connected with what is open. Otherwise, extra void should be provided between uniform and changeless elements in order to create rhythm. Each solid form or each environment, to be lively, is supposed to be self-contented in balance and equilibrium.

Nevertheless, the incorporation of solid forms and the connection between environments are not composed for purely aesthetic effect. They have their functional and psychological significances.

"Thirty spokes are assembled by one hub;
by their non-being a wheel is formed." (CHAP. 11)

Laotzu never strays from his idea of insufficiency in individual things. Again and again, he tries to emphasize the organic relationship between things, not the things themselves. Obviously, in relation to our mind, the being of one thing is always made possible by the non-being of another thing. Within the dimension of time, independent ideas cannot exist concurrently unless they are generalized and become a synthetic abstraction. The meaning of a whole and a part will concurrently exist in our mind only when we think about the relationship between them instead of about the things themselves.

The word relationship is important because it reveals the fact that a part is lively primarily due to the power of its intangible content. Without its relation with the sources of supply, a city is not a city. Without its relation with the surfaces which receive its light, a lamp is not a lamp.

By so thinking, we may realize that even an empty volume of space along a river bank could become a wharf once a footprint is engraved on its green surface. Also, we can understand why a simple memorial, which has no physical function at all, could be regarded as a part of a community so extensive in scale despite geographical demarcation. It functions as a hub.

Because of this power of insufficiency, diminution of symbolic indication in a form will not necessarily reduce its power of expression. Instead, its vitality as a meaningful being is strongly intensified by its ability to induce the mind's growing experience of the breadth or the depth of physical association.

Here lies the primary difference between imitational and original expression of the character of a building. The former presents itself immediately, gives imposition and leaves no room for human experience in time. The latter, though devoid of visual elements for abrupt association, has its suggestive content allowing for man's persuasive mind to grasp and to digest for itself.

Containing something beyond a viewer's immediate recognition, a building of original expression, particularly when it is comparatively independent in function, will be seen as something new, unreal and even queer. How, then, could a new form become visually expressive of the meaning it carries?

60

"The way to manifest is to be manifested." (CHAP. 22)

As usual, Laotzu's statement is simple and needs explanation. In order to grasp its meaning, one has to think extensively and delve deep into the domain of intangibility. Man's mind is a container of visual objects. From time to time and from place to place, he collects all objects he has seen and classifies them, either passively or actively, into different categories. All the attributes of buildings such as regional location, social relationship, size and constituency help him to know all existing forms visually at first and then by name.

But man is a living being. He looks forward. He has hope. The complete reality in his mind includes, as well as existing objects, those intangible forms which will exist in the future. Each object belonging to the future will come to him in terms of a novel form, and, because of the interaction between the objects man knows and those he does not know, the opportunity for developing the meaning of a new form is created. The reason is that although man does not know what a new container should be, he does know what it should not be. To him, the form of a new container expresses what it could be by expressing what it is not.

As is always the case for man's recognition of visual form, it is the intangible existence in man's mind or the tangible non-existence in his optical vision of other forms which determines what a specific form could be. Looking back to the past, one would realize that actually an artist's stone lion has no definite being and that it becomes and remains as one of his own only because, by distinction, it is obviously neither a tiger nor a bear.

Knowing that the being of any form is created on the basis of non-being, an architect acquires his maximum freedom of expression.

61

"The most real is revealed as unreal." (CHAP. 41)

It is very hard to clarify what is imitational and what is original in a form because things, when divorced from their names, are different in degree and not in kind. Whenever possible, however, the factor of non-being is always vital because, according to Laotzu, what may appear at the surface as something unreal actually may very well be something intangibly true. To an architect, the above quotation does not involve any thing beyond our daily intelligibility, but suggests that the total meaning of a building lies in its manifold relationship, not physical function alone.

The fact is: any existing form belongs to itself and has its temporal, spatial and personal factors of formation. Material, climate, social function, historical background and most important of all the mentalities of the persons directly or indirectly participating in the design, the execution and the use of the building are the aspects of an association conglomerated in an existing form before and after construction. The complexity of all these associations is beyond tangible representation. If a new creation does not conform with an old form in all these associations, its imitation of this old form naturally would give untrue, although realistic, presentation. Imitation is not only deadly but also dishonest simply because it expresses another thing that used to be.

Expression of composite association in architectural space requires denial of dissociable characteristics. The idea of old container for new content is impossible not merely because an old form has its aesthetic defection according to change of taste, but also because its psychological content is not parallel with a new situation. This contradiction is even more serious when the factor of differentiated association among different persons is taken into account. What is unfamiliar and new, on the other hand, has varied and perplexing but nevertheless unprejudiced meaning to all.

On its tangible side, an old form also fails in optical effectiveness. While its appearance exists in our mind, what we see becomes what we think we see so that it is mentally transformed. Our vision of a new form, being less influenced by interpretation according to previous experience, gives just the opposite effect. Good or bad as we may judge it from specific viewpoint, what is foreign and seemingly untrue to us is more likely to be true to itself. One may even say that observational dependability, the most real, is negatively secured by unfamiliarity, the unreal. Diamond could be made of fake diamond; but kiamond, an imaginary stone, always is kiamond. In new form, as in new words, falsity has no part to play.

This viewpoint of negative manifestation by uniqueness is consistent with the organic process of life. As a fact beyond argument, any life is created without a specific name and is endlessly growing beyond the signification of its name. When its being changes before it is communicated, what it is could never be told. It is something only because it is not anything else.

Like a new life, the meaning of a new building suggestively manifested by others will grow in time from nothingness to something of its own. Physically, the meagerness of its service contributing to a broader purpose gives it the potential of its functional meaning; psychologically, its visual non-being of anything else leaves it the possibility of becoming something in itself.

It is dangerous, however, to call uniqueness abstraction because any abstraction will provoke specific meaning of its own and could be easily mistaken as geometrical uniformity or structural standardization. As a result, new formalism may flourish and what used to be pure and expressive becomes a dead end and no amount of additional decoration and symbolism can save it from being monotonous and meaningless.

Perfection is unknown. Creation somehow is a matter of consciously avoiding repetition or subconsciously searching for truth. To achieve this end, assumption must be made that real abstraction is an abstraction without equivocation. Methodically, it requires unique disposition of geometrical parts penetrating into space to suggest the unique character of each building and hence to open our eyes to the new possibilities in architecture.

At this point, the problem of total harmony of different forms arises.

"The pure mind sees no flaw." (CHAP. 10)

It may or may not be possible to perceive different forms in coexistence, but there is always a possibility for them to exist simultaneously in man's mind. In a temporal sequence of larger scale, complementary similarity created by concavity, balance and equilibrium cannot satisfy man's sense of overall harmony. He wants to see the similarity between different compositions as integrated wholes instead. Turning his head laterally, focussing his optical range or walking along the longitudinal direction, man will see different objects and, if he sees them consciously, assimilate them into his memory. Even when individual compositions are separated in space, they cannot avoid man's ultimate comparison.

To a man who has the knowledge of some conventional styles simultaneously perceived or conceived by him, there is an overall diversity among them. Such a diversity appears as existing to him because his mind is categorically preoccupied by the names and the characteristics of these styles.

Here we see why Laotzu is so much for the purity and the totality of man's receptibility. To a child who is not culturally conditioned or to a man from a primitive society, categorical diversity among conventional styles does not exist. Instead, the difference among those styles only appears to him as pure variety among abstract forms. To a man who understands that all styles were created without the name of a style, the diversity superficially shown is a historical phenomenon of inevitable differentiation. As a result, he would regard this sequential variation as a natural chorus and the names of the styles as its successive verses. A learned man will mentally become a child when he sees things with an extensive scale and relative viewpoint.

Belonging to the general category of natural creation, diverse but conventional styles will appear harmonious to mentalities either passively ignorant of any style or actively accepting differentiation as natural.

It is difficult, however, for an observer to remain mentally as pure as a child or as open-minded as an art historian. Repetition and publicity in time and uniformity in space tend to transform any form or a group of forms into what appears to be a style which, when placed in the neighborhood of other forms, inevitably creates diversity.

The all-embracing way to achieve harmony is to emphasize each building's meaningful uniqueness, the factor of non-existence of categorical characteristics. By so doing, coexistence of "novelties" or "normlessnesses" either in our perception or conception can be free from associated discrimination in terms of existing styles. Negatively but lastingly, over-all similarity is created and secured by common dissimilarity.

"Being isolated only by the range of vision and audition,
Neighboring settlements achieve their unity by individuality."
(CHAP. 80)

The most concrete and constructive point suggested by Laotzu in his book is his idea of social unity. Quite different from most concepts, his method of achieving unity depends on deliberate isolation. He thinks that isolation could help avoid unnecessary conformity between individual communities and provide unity without active contact. Consistent with the general line of his thinking, this emphasis on isolation is a reaffirmation of the importance of personal tolerance, non-interference of others and the individual's freedom within intangible limitation.

The social aspect of this line of thinking is beyond an architect. The practicality implied in it, however, is useful. In functional aspect alone, privacy and solitude of life in each of neighboring buildings will be preserved by the emptiness between them.

Visually a unique form cannot be separated from the voids necessary for its intangible content. The setbacks for creating brightness contrast and fusion of surface quality, the convexity

65

for contrast and the concavity for complement between different shapes, the intangible balance of mass and equilibrium of environment all reveal their richness in and by void. But this is not all. Man's experience of more extensive-scale composition, as we have said, is not definite. Its formation depends on spatial integration in external incorporation as well as on temporal continuity in mental organization. For the control of man's subjective experience along the continuity of objective references, conscious adjustment of sequential change and transition is determined by the total grouping, deliberately arranged or otherwise, of all elements existing in space.

Deliberate incorporation of different compositions requires that in any visual arrangement although existing elements are not parts of a project, they must be regarded as parts of a total composition. Up to the level of single solid and attached solids, psychologically parts are assimilated into an organic whole by being pushed together in our optical field or circle of interest. This automatically requires the exclusion of the elements of neighboring compositions. Naturally, the clarity of individual silhouettes is reinforced by the empty space between them. In order to acquire this effect, the spacing between the parts within any individual form must not exceed the spacing between individual forms.

Similarly, for clarity of seeing toward a distance in a visual field, longitudinal depth is needed. An object which is well separated from another one in distance will be seen as individually clear and definite in contrast to the vagueness of those isolated elements which, no matter what they are, will become blurred in distance when our eyes do not focus on them.

At the level of environment organization, the unity of one group of buildings depends on both lateral spacing and longitudinal depth. At this level, other factors being equal, any single opening of an environment must be smaller than the width of surrounding space surrounding the group.

This method of acquiring visual unity by successive increase of surrounding space is applicable in any higher level of visual organization. Knowing that any cluster of stars is formed by their surrounding emptiness, one must not deny the fact that the unity between San Francisco and New York City is formed by the two oceans and not the railroads.

It is obvious that unity does not always require physical continuity and could be achieved by relating tangible forms in proximity by a common void. But the word proximity hardly defines the real condition of spatial unity. Instead, it implies possible suppression of individual forms or the formations of smaller group of forms on one hand and disregard of any combination of these units at higher organization levels on the other. It further implies that elements in context could only be deliberately related. Organic unity created by surrounding space is achieved, quite invisibly but naturally, by an innate respect for each element and its unbounded possibility for vital development and combination. Emphasis on surrounding space can thus preserve the unique status of an individual form or a group of forms built at random and also combine it with other entities which together give vital environmental organization within the process of growth.

This conscious spacing between individual forms can achieve more than visual unity and clarity. As we have mentioned, a free space seen from many viewpoints in time would have a multiplicative value much beyond its mere physical quantity and appearance. In a visual sense, proper allowance for space between and around buildings would inherently allow for man's experience of richer variety from changing points of view and fuller understanding of an architectural composition.

When the significance of unity by surrounding space is recognized by an architect, he can enjoy the maximum freedom of composition as a composer dealing with form and space. Instead of putting architectonic forms in the whole available space of a building site, he will preserve a commensurate margin between the construction line and the property line. This shrinkage of construction area is profitable. The architect is not likely to have to consider the tangible relationship with some incompatible forms in the neighborhood or unknown arrangement in the future.

In view of the fact that crowded massiveness in architecture usually symbolizes the decline of human progress, the natural space so preserved should be recognized as a living, life giving and creative vacancy for growing and transitional replacement in the future. During the period between transitional re-creations, nevertheless, it will naturally be filled with trees, flowers or lawns of indefinite quality. The factor which they form is, like greyness and void, an intangible common denominator that integrates the conception of unity and makes it free from the rule of common module.

For all architectural arrangements, the common denominators of unity in space and that of harmony of forms are the two intangibles existing in the mind of every creator and every viewer. When each building contains these two factors, surrounding space and uniqueness, it will become a lively entity because, like life, physically it radiates in space and psychologically its meaning grows in time through its functional affiliation.

CONCLUSION

THE apparent points covered in this investigation are by necessity abstractly and sporadically presented. The nature of the subject is such that a too analytical and tangible approach would tend to make the idea fade. However, throughout this investigation, the line of thinking is consistent: namely, the existence of intangible content in architectonic form.

As an additional point brought up in the introduction, readiness of functional space is interpreted as that which gives man the chance to act freely without time limitation. In the discussion of the inherent aspects of vision, endless incompletion of natural transformation and the deficiency of our visual organism are both accepted as natural assets. With the same assumption, the richness in fragmentary arrangement and the complementary shapes are emphasized.

The point has been made that physical and visual balance may both be achieved better with the help of intangible elements. This method of using intangible means to achieve a positive end is most vitally recognized as the way to acquire the human quality of growth in man's physical environment.

Intangible content in architectural composition can be said to exist as a general binder of the non-being and the being of any visual entity. Thus, it seems that when an architect composes, he is considering interdependently the invisible content as well as the tangible form.

All the methods of visual arrangement suggested in this investigation, as has been said, are the means and not the end. What an architect is asked to say and wants to say will be combined, modified, and then fused into the character of a building or a group of buildings. The ways to express this character are many, but to be honest to its incompatible psychological associations, it must be unique.

Thus, concurrently, a unique way of expression will contribute the basic requirement of normless quality for its harmony with many other buildings coexisting in natural space.

All these mean that when an architect wants to express an idea without creating any confusion in presentation and contradiction with neighboring forms, the first thing he should do is to know what not to do. As to the architect's relationship with a client who is looking for some new significance, an architect probably would have to know what the client does not want because what he does want usually could not be told.

The means for architectural composition is something conceivable. To achieve the end of a composition concerns personal creativity and is beyond our knowing. It seems, however, that Laotzu's thinking is also helpful in this respect.

> *"The way to learn is to assimilate.*
> *The way to know is to forget."*
> (CHAP. 48)

Consistent with the philosophy of non-being, to forget is regarded as an affirmative and constructive action. This is obvious to anyone who has experience in creative work. It is so, not only because we believe that there is a creative power existing in our subconscious mentality, but also because the more forgetful a man is, the less he will be inhibited by his knowledge which may and may not be helpful in a new problem.

Knowing that the living part of nature exists in void, one would believe that knowledge is subordinated to creative forgetfulness. Analogously, knowledge is similar to solid, creative forgetfulness is similar to void. They are both needed for the construction of a creation, but each has a different contribution to make. In the infinite garden of creative forgetfulness where the soil is fresh and resourceful, one will find countless possibilities for a composition. Knowledge is profitable but usually of such rigid formation that one's creative imagination and thinking cannot act freely within its limitation. Similar to the relationship between void and solid, knowledge can always penetrate into the emptiness of creative forgetfulness. While materially man moves and sees through void, mentally he imagines and thinks through creative forgetfulness.

Art is artifact that grows. Unlike science which gives form to what is formless, art releases what is artificially captured. From a positive point of view, it is right to say that form usually follows function. In order to release aesthetic and character expression from the prison of functional formalism as well as to tolerate physical limitation, it is equally profitable to know that human adaptability has no definite limit and that function may well follow form. It is when rationality and irrationality compromise each other that the art of architecture acquires its first liberty of growth.

Although the fruit of knowledge, reasoning, could be used as a means to guide imagination at the subconscious state of creation, if knowledge itself is utilized at the conscious state to frame and mould the form envisioned, it should be fused with creative forgetfulness.

Creative forgetfulness is shallow and empty at its face value. Its infinite treasure is concealed in its ever-exploratory depth of freedom. An architect who wants to compose a building that is unique and honest must, therefore, know not only what not to do, but be willing to travel without fear in the vague, winding, dark and unsure area of creative forgetfulness,—imagination.

Deep and rich as creative forgetfulness is, it is by no means the fountain of perfection. Inasmuch as to expect perfection

71

means to predict the end of creation, what an architect is sweating for is only his least undesirable product. Rather, it is his heart so incarnated which will transcend the work of his mind.

Yet man's creation, no matter how impressive and how durable, is bound to vanish from this world. Regretful is the architect who discovers that even his name, if it can endure at all, does not authentically represent himself. Without admitting the existence of spiritual life and regarding the vanishing of his tangible being as a positive contribution to humanity, an architect is not likely to acquire his real satisfaction.

Intangible content gives life-quality to architectonic form; creative forgetfulness gives life-quality to architecture; and spiritual being gives life-quality to life itself. Of these three aspects of non-being, intangible content in architectonic form is the subject of this investigation. Creative forgetfulness and spiritual being are mentioned because only through the integration of the three does knowledge acquire its significance.

The life-quality of architecture, like the life-quality of humanity itself, exists not only in the realm of the material but also in the realm of intangibility, the realm that each man must find and conquer for himself.